ONE THOUSAND THINGS

WIDE EYED EDITIONS

CONTENTS

Can you spot Little Mouse in every scene?

4

FIRST

things to learn

CAN YOU NAME YOUR COLORS?

pink

red

purple

brown

yellow

aqua

blue

olive

navy

orange

gray

green

rose

7

CAN YOU COUNT
FROM ONE TO TEN?

1

2

3

7

8

4

5

6

9

10

CAN YOU NAME THESE DIFFERENT SHAPES?

heart

circle

diamond

star

triangle

rectangle

square

11

DO YOU KNOW THESE OPPOSITES?

top

bottom

light

heavy

12

far

close

tall

short

WHAT ARE THE DIFFERENT TIMES OF DAY?

morning

night

afternoon

evening

THINGS

to do with you

WHAT ARE THE PARTS OF YOUR FACE CALLED?

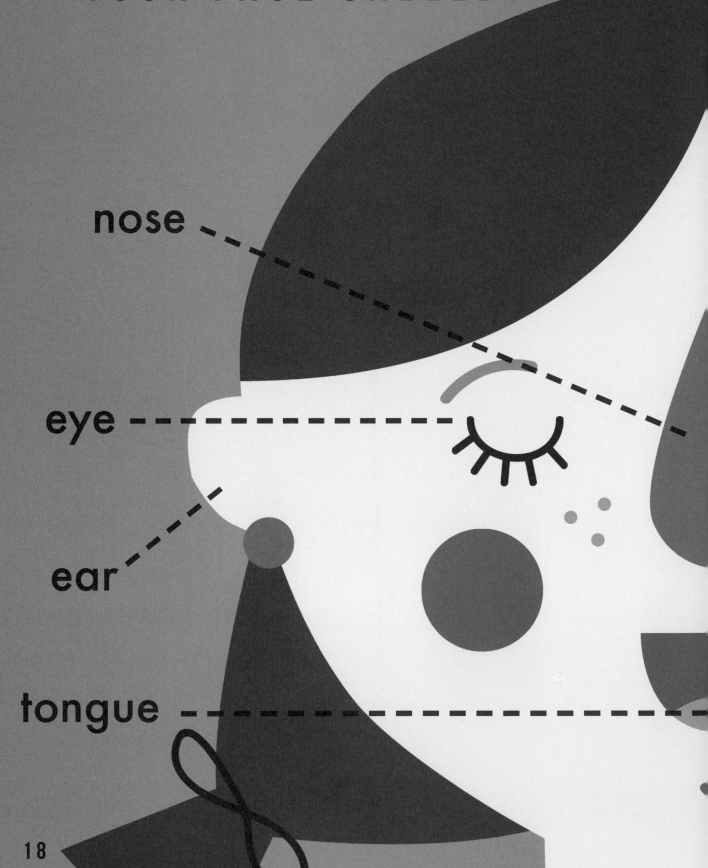

nose

eye

ear

tongue

18

hair

eyebrow

cheek

mouth

chin

19

CAN YOU NAME YOUR FIVE SENSES?

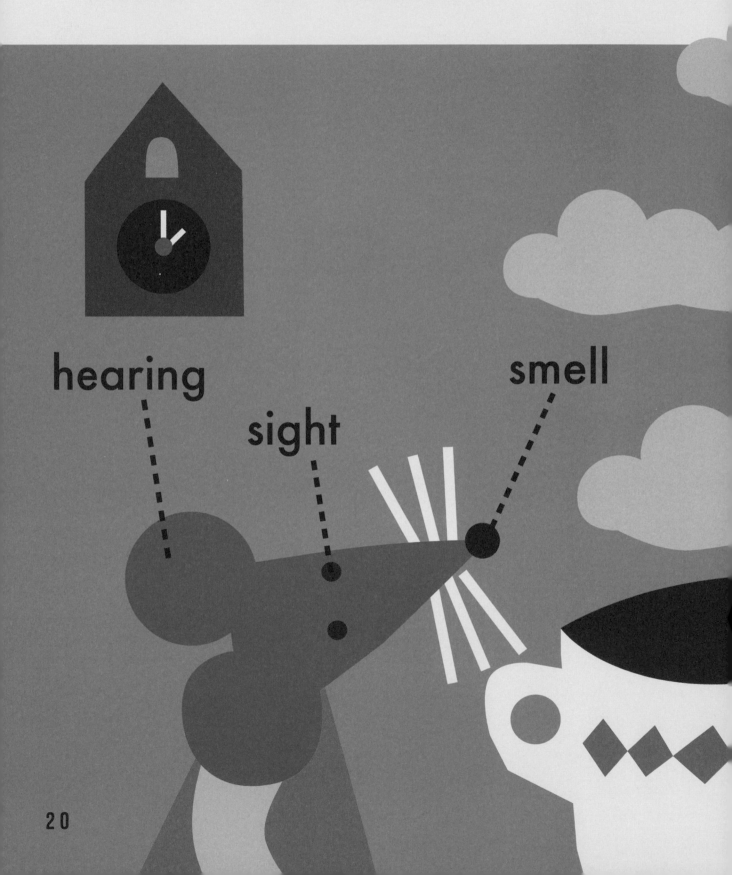

hearing

sight

smell

WHAT ARE THE DIFFERENT PARTS OF YOUR BODY?

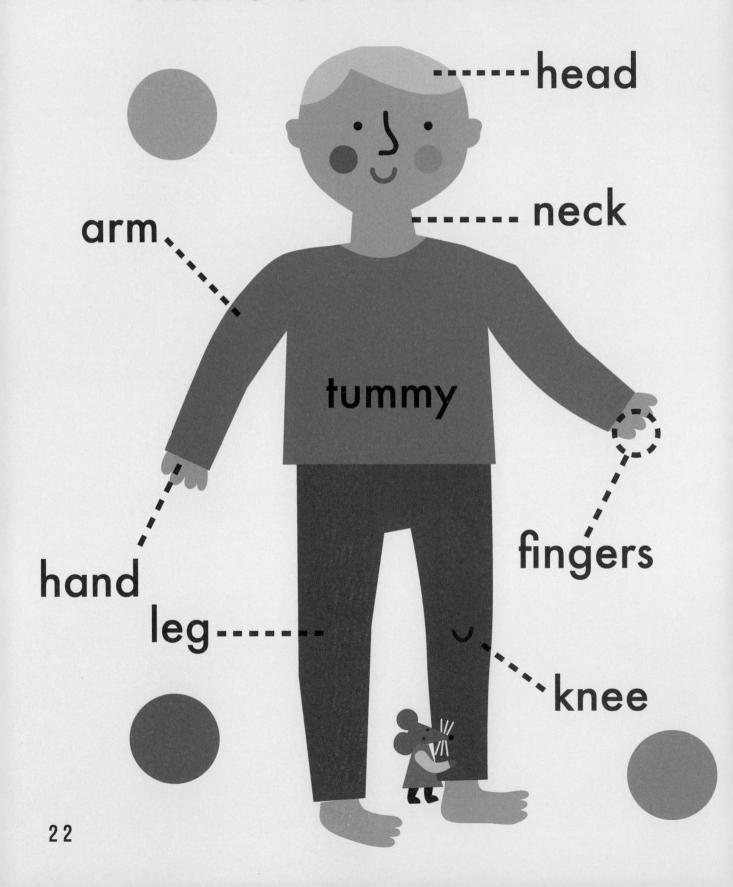

head

neck

arm

tummy

fingers

hand

leg

knee

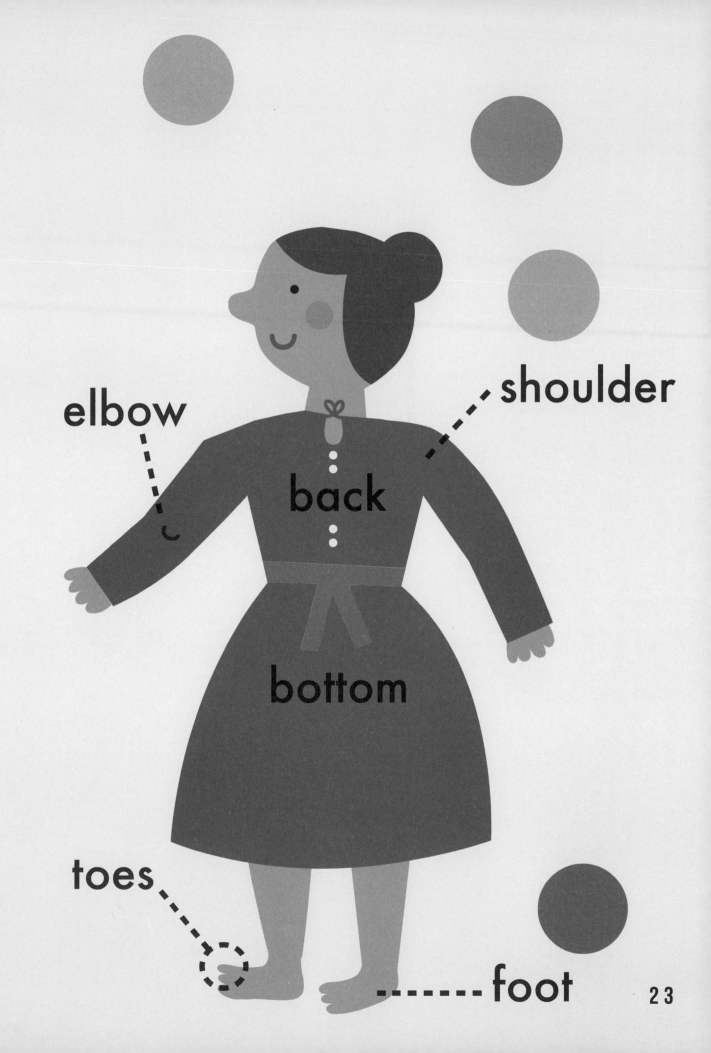

elbow

shoulder

back

bottom

toes

foot

23

WHAT WOULD YOU LIKE TO WEAR TODAY?

pants

sweater

dress

pajamas

top

glove

hat

underpants

coat

socks

shirt

shoes

25

WHO IS IN YOUR FAMILY?

cousin

dad

mom

sister

aunt

uncle

grandpa

grandma

brother

27

THINGS

around the world

WHAT ARE THE FOUR SEASONS?

spring

autumn

summer

winter

WHAT KIND OF WEATHER DO WE HAVE TODAY?

wind

WHAT CAN YOU FIND IN OUTER SPACE?

sun

moon

rocket

planet

star ------•

astronaut

THINGS

in nature

WHAT'S IN THE FRUIT BOWL?

cherry

pear

plum

apple

watermelon

mango

WHAT VEGETABLES
DO YOU LIKE TO EAT?

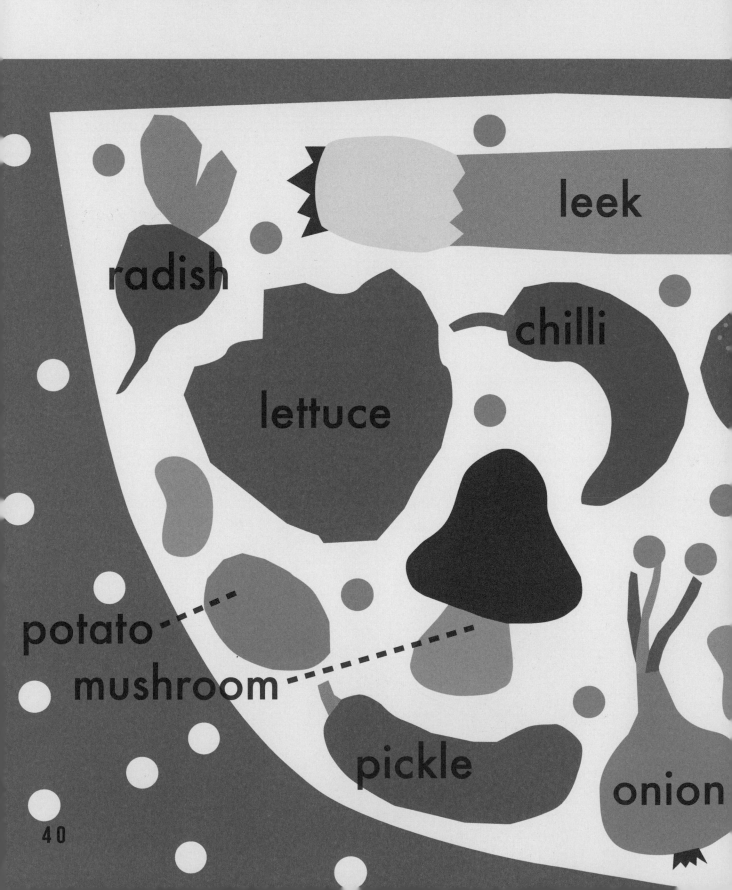

leek

radish

chilli

lettuce

potato

mushroom

pickle

onion

tomato

garlic

broccoli

cabbage

cauliflower

WHAT ANIMALS LIVE ON THE FARM?

cow

butterfly

hen

dog

sheep

bee

horse

goat

duck

pig

WHAT ANIMALS LIVE IN THE WILD?

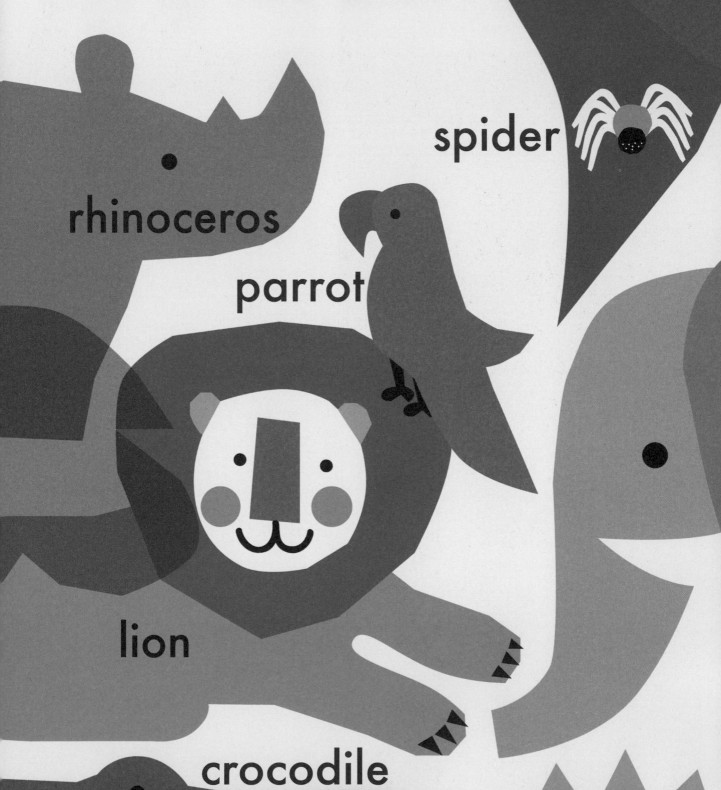

spider

rhinoceros

parrot

lion

crocodile

snake

giraffe

monkey

elephant

tiger

zebra

45

WHAT ANIMALS LIVE IN THE SEA?

octopus

fish

shark

dolphin

whale

seahorse

crab

seastar

WHAT ANIMALS WOULD YOU FIND LONG AGO?

dinosaur

saber-toothed cat ---

egg

dragonfly

mammoth

dinosaur

49

THINGS

that you can do

WHAT DO YOU LIKE
TO DO OUTSIDE?

swim

kick

dance

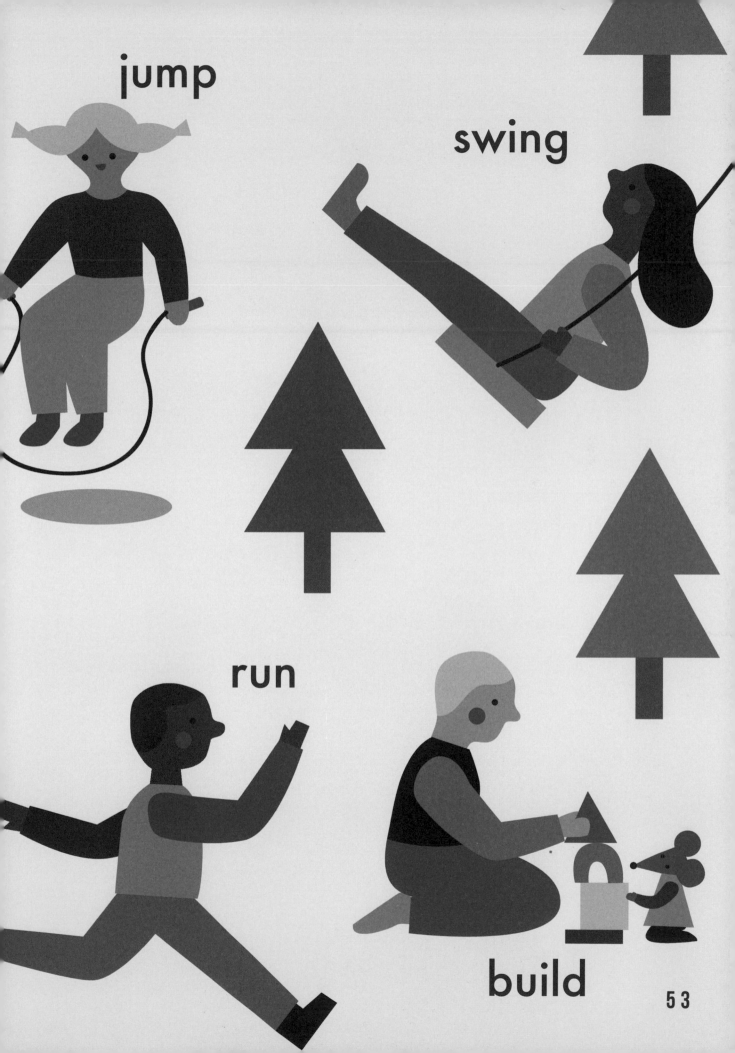

jump

swing

run

build

53

WHAT CAN YOU DO INSIDE?

read

play

paint

write

55

WHAT DO YOU DO EVERY DAY?

eat

laugh

clean

share

hug

sleep

WHAT WILL YOU BE WHEN YOU GROW UP?

artist

builder

chef

doctor

farmer

musician

teacher

vet

THINGS

inside your house

WHAT DO YOU SEE IN THE KITCHEN?

cup

saucepan

oven

fork

plate

knife

teapot

fridge

spoon

bowl

WHAT CAN YOU FIND IN THE BATHROOM?

towel

shower

sponge

bath

soap

toothbrush

toilet

WHAT CAN YOU SEE IN THE BEDROOM?

books

clock

night light

teddy

pillow

bed

toys

dresser

chair

WHAT CAN YOU FIND IN THE SHED?

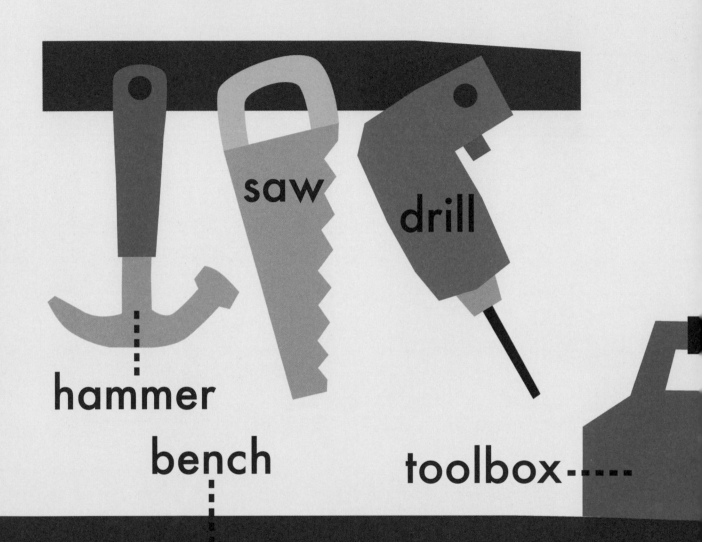

saw

drill

hammer

bench

toolbox-----

----- boots

wrench

screwdriver

nails

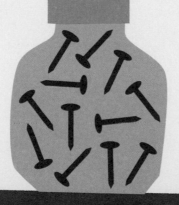

ladder

THINGS
outside your house

WHAT ARE THESE THINGS THAT GO?

tractor

car

boat

plane

bicycle

fire engine

73

CAN YOU NAME THESE BUILDINGS?

castle

tower

barn

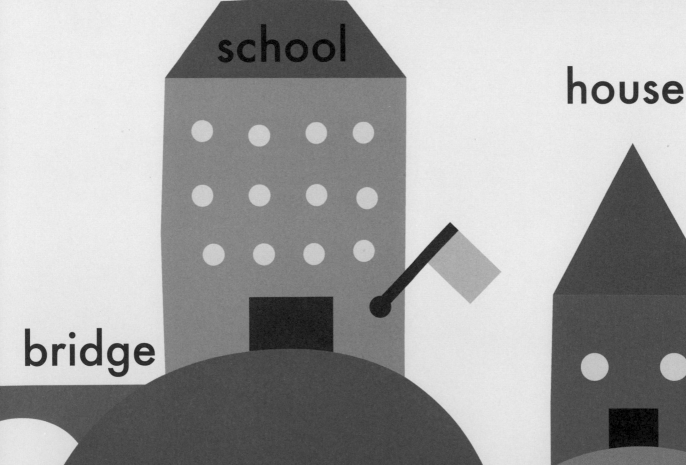

school

house

bridge

75

WHAT DO YOU SEE IN NATURE?

forest

meadow

river

mountain

tree

lake

NOW YOU KNOW HUNDREDS
OF THINGS...